Diary of a Wounded Woman

SHANTA N. SCOTT

SHANTA N. SCOTT

Dedication

This book is dedicated to ALL those that have been wounded either from sexual, verbal, physical, mental and emotional abuse.

I personally dedicate this book to my lovely lil cousin Asia Ray, I love you ladybug; my lil cousin from another family Lynette Ray a.k.a. bubbless and my gorgeous niece Brandi D. Scott, you all have been such an inspiration to me.

My lil sister Bonita Scott, who had my back when everyone turned their back on me; she has ALWAYS been my personal cheerleader on the side line for me. Love you sissy with everything in me…

My beautiful and intelligent princesses Shantez Scott a.k.a. Booda-head, A'Shantee Henderson a.k.a. Wonka-tink lady and Miracle Taylor a.k.a. Lady-bug and my prince Caleb Henderson a.k.a. Doodle-bug, b.k.a. Bam-Bam, I love you all with every being of my soul. Nothing or NO ONE will EVER change that!!!!!!!!

Acknowledgements

TO GOD BE THE GLORY IN EVERYTHING I DO FOR THE KINGDOM...

I want to thank my Apostle/Pastor/Mentor Alois Bell, who not only believed in me and my craziness but she also pushed me into the destiny that God has for me to live in. She also helped birth this book and many more to come. I thank Apostle Bell for not giving up on me and keeping hold of what the Lord has told her pertaining to me.

I also want to thank my first Pastors for over 19 years in ministry Apostle/Bishop Gregory and his wife Pastor Diane Holley. They taught me the good and the bad about ministry and how to hold on to God's unchanging hand.

I thank my mom for showing me a real woman after God's heart.

I also would like to thank Bishop Jerome and Pastor Doris Bracely for keeping me in their prayers no matter what others had to say about me.

I thank Pastor Brenda Price-Davidson for putting me in line when I was falling off the wagon.

I thank my god-sister Evangelist Yvette Johnson-Banes and my god-daughter Brittany Johnson for loving a wounded woman as I once was.

I thank my god-brother Apostle De Burney and my god-sis Pastor Belinda Ruffin who is always cheering me on to not give up and trust God above all things. God gave them to me when I was going through a rough and tough time in my life. They are truly witnesses of what the devil take away, God will surly replace. I have a BIG brother and BIG sister who love me with no strings attached…

Introduction

Are you a victim of sexual, verbal, emotional or physical abuse by family members and/or friends? Do you feel like giving up and throwing in the towel? Where does your faith reside in?

Have you been in a tough spot of hurt, humiliation, distressed depressed or even low down and dirty? I want you to know that you are not alone in this struggle. Sometimes you may not have anyone to talk to or even relate to you in your pain. I am here to let you know that I understand and have been through it too.

You may have been through MORE or less than I but it doesn't matter we are all children of the Most High God and see, knows and understand all things that we go through.

I choose to be a willing vessel that is being used from God for you all. I am the voice that will be for those that don't have one.

Forward

Starting from the beginning, just to let you know that I'm not holding anything back so there may be times when you may put this book down because of some of the gruesome pictures which may come to mind. As I go along this journey to tell my story, there are so many emotions going through my mind and body. Thoughts of: "Should I really tell this gruesome story?" " Should I tell EVERYTHING?"

"What if they get mad?"

"What will they do to me?"

"How is this going to affect my family, my children?"

So many emotions of fear, loneness, frustration, anger and even insecurities. I want to start off first by saying that I'm not seeking revenge on anyone, *I want to be healed, and help get someone to their healing through my story*. I learned that when I talk about the issues of my past, it helps me even the more to get closer to my healing and being totally delivered.

MY TEARS ARE SO BITTER, MY HEART IS SO BROKEN, DO ANYONE WHO HEARS ME...

All I am aiming to do is to help someone who may feel as if they don't have a voice in a matter. I want to be that voice.

There is power in your pain lady or man.

Chapter 1

We lived in a three bedroom home and it was 7 children in the home at that time. Starting from the age of 5-11, my biological parents (both father and mother), and brother had been molesting me. At age 11, my father attempted to rape me. My father would come into my room that I was sharing with my two younger sisters, and he would proceed to put his hands down my pants and caress my chest. This would happen just about every night. I would try to hide from him in closets, under the bed and even in my brothers' room. When he would find me, he would make me go to my bed and pull my pants down or pull my gown up so he can touch me.

MY HEART IS SHATTERED TO PIECES...

NOT SURE HOW TO MEND IT TOGETHER

I was never able to go outside and play with the other kids. I had to stay in the house and go to a room to lay down to get touched on by my father. This went on for about 4 years before my brother would started to touch me. Now, you may be asking, "Where was your mom?" Well, she was the breadwinner of the family. My father went years without a job, so she had to work to support all of us. My mother was also a church-going woman, so that left me to stay with my father many days by myself.

For just a moment, I want to speak on my brother. I love him, to this day, with every being of my heart. However, the pain has to be mended and healed. When my brother started to touch me, it was so hurtful. Although he never fully took my virginity, he rubbed his penis around that area and released himself on me. I went through this abuse from my brother for over a year, before I decided to tell on both my father and my brother.

I was going back and forth with the both of them, in the morning or afternoon my brother then at evening time with my father. At that point in my life, I was wondering "What is going on?" and "Why is this happening to me?" I never in my heart thought that this was right. It didn't feel right but I didn't know how to stop it. I was wishing and hoping that they would stop, or even that someone would find them and catch them. Whew what a time to live huh?

TRYING TO UNDERSTAND THE PAIN

INSIDE...BUT I HEAR NO VOICE TO TALK

FOR ME...

During this same time, we had a cousin, on my father's side of the family, to stay over our house. When the kids would play games, like hide-and-seek, he was play hide and seek with the younger kids but had me to stay by him. He put my hands on his penis and he put his hand down my pants. I did as he told me because he was bigger and older than I was.

I began to think maybe I deserved this. Maybe I was being punished for something. Maybe I was to go through this because I was the oldest girl in the house, so this is normal. These were the thoughts running through my mind. Now I can remember being 10 years old when this particular incident happened. Now that only happened once but I was feeling like here I go again, wondering does he know something? So I never ever told anyone about him until now also. Not to hurt him but because he is part of the story and pain also. He has AIDS now. I still pray for his healing because even in this process. I don't want anyone to go to Hell without repenting, turning from their wicked ways and get help from God. NO ONE.

THE DARKNESS IS STARTING TO

SURROUND MY BROKEN HEART...

There was other cousin is on my mother's side of the family. I was around 8 years old. One day I was visiting my aunt with my mom ,who was his mom. While they were in the back talking, he called me to sit and watch TV with him, and I did. He sat on one couch and I was about to sit down in a chair. Before I could even sit down, he told me to come by him. He unbuckled my pants and t his hands went down my pants. No, I never told my mom. I was starting to really believe maybe this is why I was born: to have all these men get off. He now is in prison for the rest of his life, the last I heard.

I said to myself one day, "If it happens tonight, again, then I am telling someone." Of course it happened again: first my brother, then my father. That next day, I went to my mom and told her what was happening between me, my father and my brother. I heard her go to confront my dad. I heard him tell my mother I was lying on him. I heard my brother tell her that he didn't know what he was doing was wrong because he saw my farther do it to me so he thought it was okay. Now you will see further why I had to start speaking about my brother later.

THE SPLIT WAS DEEPER THAN I COULD

IMAGE...NOT JUST ONE BUT TWO...

Of course I never blamed my brother for what he had done to me. Even to this day. It still hurts because even knowing that he saw my father do those things to me, he never thought to stop him. He thought it was okay to hurt me more. I know that you are wondering by now, "Why are you talking about your brother now if you never blamed him?" Here is the reason why. I must get totally healed in order for me to go any further in ministry. Even if I never go further in ministry, I want to be healed just for me.

Although I never blamed him, there was always a thick tension between the both of us. Many may not understand that choosing to live a life of anger, frustrating relationships with men and hold all sort of unanswered questions in your heart AND still blame yourself for things that you couldn't control will never help you heal. I want to be free from living that sort of life. And if telling my story helps me, I'm sure it will help you 'come out from under the bed' as well.

THE WINGS OF MY HEART IS FULL OF

ANGER AND DEMONS...

ANYONE HEAR MY CRIES...

Chapter 2

At times we would get into arguments as we got older, and a few times he told me I was the blame for breaking up the family by sending his dad to jail. When I would say things like "You was the cause of my hurt and pain too", but still never openly spoke on it. I held on to those words for years, and it tormented my soul spirit. This is why I made the decision to unleash the hurt from both my soul and spirit to be put back together as a woman. At that time, I wasn't a woman. I was operating as a damaged soul.

To be healed and whole, I had to deal with the broken pieces that were missing deep down in my soul. Although I never blamed my brother because of what I heard him tell my mom, when I found out that it was wrong, it still hurt within. I lived a life of shame and regret. The two most important men in my life, who are to love and protect me from the world, were the two that was using me for their own selfish desires. They were abusing the body that was innocent in the beginning and hurting me in this world.

Now stay with me I maybe going back and forth in my story, but I promise you will not be lost. My dad was making me watch pornography, and telling me as it will show me 'how to be a woman' and 'what to do to keep a man'. Those were the very words were, "You aren't worth anything but to open your legs and do these things to keep a man." Yep. I remember that sentence like it was told to me yesterday. These very words ran through my mind so many times as I was growing into my womanhood. *These words penetrated my soul to the point I believed them, and my actions showed it.* You may be asking "Why you would believe something like that?" Well, it came from my dad. I believed everything my dad told me.

JUST SITTING IN THIS WORLD WITH NO

DAD TO LOVE ME

This was why it was so hard to trust men with my feelings. It became the reason I became ill-feeling, angry, hateful, disloyal to men.

I remember times when my brother would threaten me if I wouldn't let him do things to me. He said that he would harm me with his fist and I didn't want to get hit so I just laid there and allowed those things to hurt me. So, this helped me to build a wall of bricks up against men to keep from ever being hurt again.

As a child growing up in these awful things, I was started to believe that I wasn't meant to live. I will never be worth a wife, or even a girlfriend. I hated my younger siblings and wishing that these things would happen to them, and then I would have some freedom. I didn't understand the anger that was brewing in my heart, but I did know that it was getting worse every day I encountered these two men.

I never told about these cousins because I just felt like there was no help coming my way, so I never told. But, now I'm getting released from every hidden hurt, every hidden pain that resides in me. Dealing with my father and brother at home, it scared me to the point that for many years I never had the guts to look at a male figure in their eyes. I became a mute, even in school. My grades started to go left. I only came home with D's and F's, ON PURPOSE.

THE FANTASIES START...I'M

DREAMING OF A BETTER LIFE ONE DAY...

I started to act out in school. I did this because I was searching and reaching for attention. School was really hard for me, I had to get touched before going to school and I felt nasty. I was at my wits end one day and I think he knew. I would start to do things to stop him from touching me. I would pee in the bed. I wouldn't change my messy bloody pads while on my period, thinking it would drive him off me. However it didn't, he would just tell me to change the sheets and or go get in the tub and get cleaned. Many times he would watch me take a bath, as if he wanted to be sure I was clean.

JUST A LOST YOUNG SOUL WITHERING IN THE DARKNESS OF LIFE...

THIS NIGHT RIGHT HERE KILLED MY SOUL AND STRIPPED MY HEART.

One day, I even thought I seen and heard my mom ask him what he was doing in my room. He said that he was either closing the window or just putting the girls to bed, something to that affect. I'm not sure if that even happened. I seem to not be able to remove that image from my memory. I never asked my mom if she knew, but I always wonder how she could *not* know? My father had told me that if I was to tell, that no one would believe me. Pedophiles tell their victims those very words. Don't think that the child is just being silly, or you don't understand why it took so long to tell. It takes a lot of guts to tell someone after hearing those words 'no one will believe you'. My father also told me that I would hurt the family, and they would hate me. Now hearing those words coming from my father ,who I still adore and love because that's my father, I never wanted my family hurt. So I told myself I would just keep it to myself.

At this point I was just existing, but not living.

ALL DREAMS ARE SHATTERED WITH

THE SPEAR OF HOPELESSNESS...

Chapter 3

I had so many mixed emotions about what was happening to me in that little house. I believe that house is still standing right at this very moment. As a matter of fact it is and I still don't have the guts to just look at the house. As if it was the house fault for what was going on there almost 34 years ago (just a lil joke). Even at this moment in my life were I'm no longer going to be bound up with past secrets of the family which would keep myself from getting totally healed and set free from my pain to become a better person, it still haunts me. I have dreams about the both of them at times. I even smelled my father at times, and just cried because I want to be whole and get released from these issues.

When I look at my brother and knowing that he has daughters of his own, I wonder does he think about me. Does he wish he could change back time and apologize? Or does he just wish I was dead (as he would tell me sometimes?). Even with writing this book to encourage someone else to speak up and get released from your hurts, it still hurts. However, I will go forth through the pain and the hurts. If me getting stones thrown, name slandered, reputation slaughtered to help you get healed and delivered for real? Then let it be. I'm so serious. I'm so tired of women and men being taunted with the pain of their past even in the present.

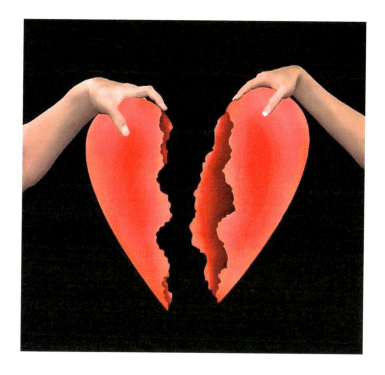

TWO OF THE MOST IMPORTANT PEOPLE TORE MY HEART APART...WILL THOSE TWO BE ABLE TO MEND IT BACK...

Chapter 4

My dad was and still is an alcoholic and drug user. He always smells like alcohol. The last I heard, using heroin and crack. I didn't know at that time this was happening he was using drugs and alcohol. I found out later in life. He has been on drugs even before I was born, is what I was told.

As I said earlier, there were 7 of us in the home. Yep I'm the second oldest, so I have 5 siblings under me (4 now because the brother who helped me died in the year 2001). **Rest. In.**

Heaven.

LOVE YOU ARTHUR B. SCOTT JR.

NOONE WILL EVER REPLACE YOU***

LEARNING HOW TO PATCH THE

HEART UP...

BUT STILL NOT HEALED...

For many years I blamed myself for his murder because he didn't have his father in the home which ran him into the hands of gangs and drugs. But God told me in a dream that it wasn't my fault and for me be released from that bondage. So you might say, "Then why didn't God tell you to get released from this bondage of hurt and pain?" It's easier to forgive yourself or even someone else when they are out of sight. My father and brother was always in sight. So it was so hard for me to move on at that time.

But God has a way of getting your attention when He wants it.

With dealing with the both of them, I was beginning to reach my breaking point. I became numb to feelings as I got older. I started to hate myself so my self- esteem was shot to the ground. Because I felt abandoned and rejected by those that I felt was to protect me from harm, I started to hate authority.

THE DRIPPING OF HATRED AND

BITTERNESS...THE DRIPPING OF

LONELINESS AND INSECURITIES...

As I continued to attend school, I had friends who would talk about their fathers, big brothers, uncles and cousins and the things they have done for them it started to bother me to the point I hated my friends. I pushed them away from liking me. I started to feel alone and helpless. I cried many nights asking the air, not knowing I was talking to God, to help me and get rid of these things that are hurting me. At the age of 11, before I was removed from my mother's house, I ran away from home many times and never had anyone to look for me. I even went to school from the girl's house that I ran to and later just showed up at home without a question asked.

I cried to the air asking why these things are happening to me. I even asked the air to kill me many times. I started to think that I was getting treated this way because I was the ugly duckling. For many years I couldn't read that story of the ugly duckling because it would remind me of me and my situation. I didn't like my face, the color of my skin, my lips because they are big, my nose, my legs because they were hairy. I just hated myself and had no one to tell me that I was beautiful. My low self-esteem carried over into in my marriages.

WHAT YOU SEEN POSTED ON MY FACE.

BEWARE OF THE DANGER APPROACHING...

I remember my father giving me money to touch me, but of course I had nowhere to spend it. He would take it back and tell me that I would get it the next time. I also remember my father braiding my hair, and on many days and he would thrust himself against my back. He would ask me if I felt that and if I wanted it. One day after he braided my hair, after he said those words to me he went to the bathroom. As soon as I had a chance, I ran out the house as fast as I could. Our neighbor saw me and brought me back to the house. I still never said anything. She didn't know I was running for my life. She thought I was being rebellious to my parents and bought me back home.

The molestation started to become normal for me. I would come home from school and get molested by my brother then later on, my father.

TWISTED FAITH NOT

NOTICED...

One day as my mother went to church, and I was left at home as usual, my dad thought that he would go a little further with me. He called me into his room, telling me to take off my clothing and he started to kiss me. I was confused because he never kissed me before, and I was scared. He started pulling down his pants and told me to relax. "It will be over in a minute." he said. He told me to touch his penis, and rub it. It felt like forever and a day. I felt him pushing into me. It was hurt, and I told him that. He would put his lips on mine to hush me from getting louder. Right at the moment, I believed if he wasn't stopped, I was going to be raped by my father. It was my younger brother who he intervened. He opened the door, screaming from the top of his lungs "WHAT ARE YOU DOING TO HER?" My father jumped off me and ran out the room to get my little brother. I ran into my room and locked the door. At that time I had this big piano organ. I pulled the organ against the door. My dad came to my door telling me to open the door so he can finish what he started. I was scared out my mind. I once again began to climb out my bedroom window and a friend from across the street seen me. He told me he would help me out. Right at the moment he was coming across the street, my mom was walking down the street then he stopped.

HOPELESSNESS HAS ENTERED...

Now please don't get it twisted. I love my mom with everything that is in me. Do I wonder if she blames me for her husband going to jail and leaving her to raise 7 kids alone? Yes, I carried that pain too. As you can imagine we all went through some awful things in these streets. Many of us were gang members, sold drugs, stole cars and many other things. So I know it was hard for her to try to raise 7 kids all by herself. Now, does it hurt that she was the next person that I was depending on to protect me, and she wasn't that person? Of course it hurt. It drove me to hate older women because I felt like my mom never helped me, so another woman can never say a word to me or it would be a problem.

I targeted older women to fight because of my pain. I disrespected older women. I didn't care if it they were in authority or just a woman walking the streets. However, two women got close to my heart and I very well appreciate them to this day. My teacher for two grades (6th and 8th)Mrs. Dorsey and Mrs. Vera Brookes. Also, my friend's grandmother may she rest in paradise.

Chapter 5

At that moment I said I need to stop this. So one night I told my mom what both my dad and brother were doing to me, while she was gone to work or at church. I heard her ask my father if he did that to me and of course he said I was lying, my brother said he saw my dad do it so he thought it was ok to do. I thought if he seen it, why didn't he help me like my little brother did?

LIFELESS MOMENTS...

I was just at the end of my rope with this. When I finally got tired, I was 11 ½ years old in the 6th grade. One day, in class (I will never forget this), my teacher Mrs. Dorsey, (my 6th grade teacher), she was teaching on being touched in our private areas and what we need to do if this was happening to us. I didn't say anything at that moment because I was still kind of confused as to what to do or say, because it was happening to me from two people: my father who I adored, and my brother who I loved.

I took my teacher aside and told her the things that were being done to me in my home. She instantly called the social worker at the school. I was in a room along with the police telling this

gruesome story again. The social worker asked me if my father

was at home right now. I told her "Yes and my mom may be there

also." I had no idea what was going to happen next. I'm kind of

glad they didn't tell me because I believe I would have told them

that I was lying because I never wanted to hurt my mom. I just

wanted the touching and things to STOP!

HEARTS FULL OF

DISTRUST...

I was taken to my home and told to go in and get some clothes. I remember my mom face to this day when she opened the door and saw me with the police and a social worker. Her face had a frown on it and her lips were poked out staring at me, as to say "What have you done?" The police instantly went into the house and escorted my dad out and I was sent in to get my clothes. The kids were all crying and asking what was going on. I felt so bad. "But what was I supposed to do now?", I was thought. I see the police say some things to my dad and the social worker said some things to my mom. I was sitting in the back of the police car looking at my little sisters and brothers just crying and yelling where they taking her? After that I didn't see them anymore for a year or two.

Yep, this story is going before my eyes as if it was happening yesterday. I remember it so clear and still as I'm typing as the tears keep rolling down my face. "What kind of life is this to live for a little girl?" I never, ever in my whole life wanted to have kids of my own because I wasn't sure that I could protect them. I never thought that I would even live past the age 14.

HEART OF HATRED...

I was sent to a youth home that was located on Vandeventer next door to the Juvenile Hall at that time. I stayed there for maybe 6 months. While I was there, I lived with 2 other girls in a room. Even here, we all were being touched by the janitor. He would come into our room that we shared and told us he knew why we were in the home. He said he would protect us from those men out in the streets if we would let him touch us, so we let him. Once again we knew it was wrong, but never told anyone. This went on the whole 6 months that I was there. I left before the other girls, so I'm not sure if he kept touching them or not.

So now it's time for us to go to court. The social worker wanted to put my brother in jail also, but I told her that I will not talk against him because he didn't know what he was doing to me. She was so mad at me. I stood on my word that I would not send my brother to jail. I protected him all my life. I just always had it in my mind that he was innocent too. So he was never sent to juvenile. Yes, I actually went to court with a defense and prosecuting attorney and judge. I saw my mom, grandmother, my father's mother and my father. I was put on the stand to speak on the issues. As I started to tell my story, I thought that would be easy and it's finally time to stop. Then the defense attorney had his time with me. When I say the movies are so real about how they badger the victims and try to confuse them on their story!

SOLID HEART OF RESCUE,

I THOUGHT...

He was asking me so many questions, and I couldn't keep up with him. At the end of me talking, I thought what I went through didn't happen to me for real. I started crying and crying and at that point the judge stopped the questioning. My father stood up pleaded guilty instantly at that moment. I watched the police handcuff my dad and walk him off. Now, was the time of rights. The judge said some things and then I went off with my mom and the social worker. The social worker told me that I was going to live with my grandmother for a while. Even then, as I look back now I had the gift of discernment. I begged them not to send me with her and to take me back to the home. All I was thinking at that moment was, "That's my dad mother. I don't know her. She will hate me." And it was the truth. The social worker told me I didn't have a choice in the matter and this was what my mom wanted.

I lived my next part of pain in the home of the grandmother who I never was raised around so I didn't really know her. I'm going to try to not say too much about her because she has passed away and that pain has been removed. I really don't know how she felt, but her actions showed me that she didn't like me. I was called names like 'bitch' and 'whore'.

GREEN HEART IS LIFE,

I THOUGHT...

I had an aunt who, for whatever the reason, is even now had hate for me. She lied on me many times and always tried to get me into trouble with my father's mother. My father's mother never asked me how I felt about what had happened to me or even told me that she felt bad for what happened to me. Yes, she was getting a check for me by the state but she never helped me with it. My mom still had to come and buy me clothes and necessities.

Now I can't tell you actually the time that my dad was sent to prison because I remember when I was staying with his mother he came to visit. Everyone knew what was going on with him and he was still able to come to the home of the woman who the state and my mom sent me to. He actually even over there tried me. One day he was over there and everyone was outside on the porch. He told me to come sit between his legs. No one said anything but at that time I started to feel something rise up in me and I said "NO!" HE LOOKED AT ME AND ROLLED HIS EYES. After that day I never saw him again for 7 years. However, I stayed with his mother for one year and it was the 2nd worst time in my life.

She told me one day that I lied on her son. That was my breaking point once again. I yelled at her and slapped her out her chair and I ran for my life. I ran down the street and a young man that I knew down the street seen me running and he took me to my mom house. From that day I was reunited with my siblings and mom.

BLUE HEART IS NEW

BEGINNING, I THOUGHT

Before I start talking about going home to my mom, let me take you back a few.

During that year living with my father's mom I encountered a lot of things in my life. I was in school one day in the 8th grade and this young man name Michael saw me coming from the bathroom. He trapped me in the janitor's closet and he was trying to rape me. But this time I screamed and the janitor came to my rescue. Michael was suspended and expelled from school. I made up in my mind that I was not going to let this happen to me again. I met a lot of guys and this was the time that all emotions started to arise in my soul. Some I liked and some I didn't like.

Chapter 6

I had my first boyfriend at the age 13. He was 16 years old. He made me feel like I was special and protected. He told me one day that he knew the things that my father did to me from his uncle. He only knew this because his uncle and my father were in jail together. I don't know how it goes in jail, but it seems as if everyone will eventually know why you're there. I found out his uncle was incarcerated with my father at the same time and that he told my boyfriend what had happened to me.

PURPLE HEART IS ROYALTY,

NOT WORTHY...

At that time, my boyfriend told me that he would protect me and he wouldn't let anything to happen to me. I trusted him with everything that was in me. I was dating him for 6 months when one day he asked me to follow him to his friend's house. I never thought anything was wrong, because I trusted him.

As we approached the friend's house, I had seen my aunt. The same aunt who always had a problem with me. I also saw my cousins with their boyfriends at the time. They were all in the front of the house talking. We went into the back of the house and everything still seemed to be alright because I knew all the guys and I trusted them all.

As I entered the house from the back door, I was thrown onto a mattress that was one the floor. I saw my boyfriend and four of his friends. My boyfriend pulled my pants down, while two boys were trying to open my legs. As he was trying to get on top of me, I felt a strength come over me. I tell you the truth I have no idea where that strength came from. I held my legs closed and I fought for my life. I never screamed not sure why either. I remember like it was yesterday. My boyfriend said this to me, "I know you not a virgin. Just let us do this, and it will be over." I felt used like a rag. They all were starting to get frustrated and called another male in to have more hands on me.

YELLOW HEART IS LIGHT, I NEVER

HAD WITHIN...

It seemed to go on forever and a day. I was starting to get tired of fighting and that very moment I was about to give up, my aunt's boyfriend came in. He ran all the guys off me. He told me to pull my clothes up and go home and he dared them to touch me. He was truly and angel that helped me.

On my way home, my aunt and cousin acted like they didn't know what happened to me. I went to my grandmother's house and instead of asking if I was okay, she started calling me all sorts of names. I wanted to scream and tell her what just happened to

me, but I didn't think she would believe me or even care.
So, I stayed silent. This was the beginning of my anger, bitterness
and hatred towards men as well as older women.

One of the great things about living with my father's mother
was that I was introduced to the church life. I started to attend the
Salvation Army Christian church and I had so much fun. So
during that time I build myself up to overlook the issues of my life.
I learned how to put on a fake smile in the middle of hurt.

The guy that helped me from those cruel boys was the same
guy that seen me running from my grandmother's house and who
gave me a ride to my mom's house. I don't even remember my
mom asking me why I was at the steps of her home. All I know is
I was reunited with my mom and my siblings. I thought that
everything would be perfect now that I was home. I didn't realize
my siblings had their own feelings about what had happened.

I know I was under the guardianship of the state but no one
came after me, no one called about me. This was the beginning of
me not trusting authority.

ORANGE HEART IS HONOR,

I THOUGHT...

I was saying to myself, "Why they not looking for me?" The system failed me as it has many others. I thought I must defend for myself and I started to fall under the hands of the evil forces of this world. I told myself that I have to live and not let others hurt me by any means necessary. I will kill people if I had to. I began to believe no one will protect me. I felt like I was in this world on my own.

So many things went on between me and my siblings. Not so much the last four kids, but between my older brother and my brother that has passed away in 2001. There was so much tension between us three, but no one said anything about anything. However, every time we were had an altercation, I was always told that I was the reason for my father not being there. I was told that I needed not be in the house. I was told by both my brothers that they hated me and wished I was never came home. I started to distance myself from my other siblings because I didn't want anyone to hate me. I was also tired of fighting about what had happened to me.

The house was full of angry children that really didn't understand were the hate came from, but reacted from the hurt. We didn't fight like the average siblings did, we fought to hurt. We cussed each other out, tried to hurt each other physically.

A FAUCET OF EVIL

ENTANGLED IN ONE...

I remember a time I stabbed my older brother (Yes, the same brother was molesting me along with my father) with a fork. I never apologized about it. I wanted to kill him, literally.

As an 8th grader, living at my mom's house going to the 9th grade I started to 'feel myself', as the older generation would say. I became very rebellion towards my mom. I hated myself. I had low self-esteem, no peace in my heart. I had hatred my siblings and

I despised authority.

I got my first taste of blood with a fight with these 3 girls. Since I was the new girl at Blewett Junior High, there were many boys trying to talk to me. Of course, the girls didn't like that and some planned to fight me at the end of school one day. I was told by one of the boys what was about to happen. He gave me two school locks to fight with. I remember the girls all surrounded me at my locker calling me names. With them doing that, it took me back to my grandmother calling me out my name. This was the beginning of a hard life for me. So, I started to hang out with girls who were talking back to their parents and running away from home and worse things. Mind you I never fought before so I didn't know what to do. Before I knew it the police was holding me and when I opened my eyes the girls all had blood coming from everywhere, their mouths, noses and even their eyes were busted.

Chapter 7

As a freshman at Jennings High School, I was going to school with my older brother. Although everyone knew we were siblings, we never acted as if we cared for each other. I didn't look at him as being my big brother. I just said, "Hey that's my brother but he doesn't like me". I told everyone that even up till my adult years.

FANTASY OF LOVE,

I YEARNED FOR...

I was searching for love in all the wrong places, and everyone knew I was searching. I got involved with this gang of guys who were actually gang members. So, I portrayed myself as a gang member too. I went around throwing gang signs, speaking their language and even fighting to defend the name of the gang. Not knowing what was ahead of me for doing this. I had a rival gang member literally hating me, wanting to kill me and my friends.

The guys would try to get me jumped by girls they knew. One day they went as far as making a homemade smoke bomb and threw it on my porch, were my other siblings and mom lived. The bomb started a fire. No one knew what had happened, but I did. Now I started to stay away from home more because I didn't want anything to happen to my family because of me and what I was doing. The guys would threaten my uncle out of his money because of me.

WHERE IS THIS

GOD?

It was just so much that went on living in that house and in the same neighborhood to a rival gang member.

OUTSIDE HARDSHIPS

Let me explain a little bit. I would tell people that I have been gang raped but they never who did that to me (Now, remember earlier I told you about the boyfriend and his friends who tried to rape me, but didn't succeed). I started to date one of the gang members that I hung out with, thinking again that he would protect me and love me the way I wanted.

One day I was with him alone, and we were doing what we do, then here comes more of the gang members in the bedroom. I remembered it was like 5 of them, and they all had turns with me. I cried and asked my boyfriend why was he doing this to me. He told me to just relax. I remember crying during the whole session. They put their penises in my mouth and in my butt. Sometimes it was two at a time in me at the same time. When they were done, I got myself together and my boyfriend at the time told me not to tell or he will kill me. Once again I never told anyone not even two of my closest friends who knew I left with my guy friend but they had

no idea of what else went on in that bedroom. I STAYED

SILENT. This was my first encounter of being gang raped.

IS THIS GOD REAL?

When they were done, I got myself together and my

boyfriend told me not to tell or he would kill me. Once again, I

never told anyone not even two of my closest friends who knew I

left with my boyfriend but they had no idea of what else went on in that bedroom. I stayed silent. After that, I never spoke to him again. I stayed far away from him.

At this time in my life, from the age 13-17, I was in the streets doing absolutely whatever I wanted to do, whenever I wanted to do it, with whomever I wanted to do. I spent months at a time away from the home and I can't remember my mother ever asking me what was I doing. She never really talked to me about anything. I lost all respect for myself and others around me. My mom and I stayed at odds with each other. I never told my mom where I was going. I didn't respect myself and I didn't respect her either. I stayed out at other people's houses. I repeated that because many people don't believe that at age 13 no one was concerned about my whereabouts. Even if my mom was worried she never said anything to me. NEVER SAID ANYTHING TO ME. Or if she did, I never heard her. I had shut my ears to her at that time.

DOES THIS GOD SEE ME?

One day, I and a couple of my friends were walking late at night around 1 a.m. down Grand Blvd. I remember it like it was yesterday. A group of guys pulled beside us, pulling us in a car. We were pulled into the car, but my two friends found a way out the car. But the way I was sitting in the car, I couldn't free myself. One of my friends got stuck in the seat belt, and the guys had dragged her in the car about two blocks before they realized what they were doing and they released her. Yet, I was still stuck in the car. We kind of knew the guys only by name, but we didn't hang out with them of a lot.

After my friends were freed from the car, the driver took the other two guys wherever they wanted to go. At this same time, I was seeing a guy who was in a gang and lived in the Cochran Projects. Come to find out the guy who kidnapped me knew the guy I was seeing, and he wanted me to stop dating the boy I was seeing, and start seeing him (the kidnapper). He had some sort of strange crush on me and I never knew it. So he said when he seen us walking, he wanted to get me alone and try to convince me to leave my guy friend alone. We went to a hotel for two days and he never violated me of any way. He feed me and just talked the whole two days. Funny, huh? I thought the same thing.

THEY SAY THE BLACK HEART IS

FULL OF EVIL. I SAY THE BLACK HEART

IS FULL OF STRENGTH WITHIN...

He let me go and instead of dropping me off just anywhere he asked me where I wanted to get dropped off. I went to my friend house. My mom, even to this day, has no idea that I was kidnapped for two days at the age of 16.

This is exactly why I praise and worship God, Jesus Christ the way I do. Only because when I look back over my life and I see how he was still protecting me. These situations could have been worse.

Chapter 8

I started to jump from man to man at this time. Not caring who I hurt or who even knew about it. Although I was still seeing the guy in the projects, I was bouncing all around town (literally). I was dealing with about 5 dudes at the same time once. It was very dangerous because 4 of these guys were in gangs, they were rival gang members. If they would have known about each other, I could have been killed just because the guys would have thought I wanted to set them up.

Once again, I was caught up in so many things. I was a high school dropout in the 10th grade. I went to Lafayette High School in Rockwood School District for a very short time. I wasn't the prettiest girl, I had little to almost nothing. I didn't dress to part, and point blank I wasn't that attractive even though, I had been sleeping with a lot of men.

STRENGTH COMING IN

SLOWLY...

I had just started my first real job at Six Flags so I did start to buy clothes and do things to better myself physically when I met this guy from another gang that was enemies with the guys I was with.

I started to have small conversations with him at school and I was fascinated with him because I wasn't popular and had few friends. Well one day (and to this day I have no idea how he knew where I lived), the guy approached my house and I answered the door. He pointed a gun at my stomach and told me to get in the car or he and his friends will kill everyone in the house. I left with him in the car he had. I asked him where was we going and his only reply was, "Don't worry about it. You want to be in a gang, I will show you what we do to those girls in a gang". We ended up at his house. I remember it was very dark and quiet. I just knew I was going to get gang raped again because of the other guys in the car. Well, they never came in the house and there we went to a bedroom. I was told to take my pants off. I said no, and he tore them off me. He began to rape me over and over, while I was pleading and begging him to stop and take me back home.

STRENGTH AND LIFE

WRAPPED IN ONE...

He told me he would take me home when he gets done. He

took me home and I never saw him again, because I stopped going

to school. So I was a school drop out for about a year or so.

I can't stress this enough of how my mind went haywire. I

started to feel as my body was the cue for what men wanted out of me, and that I needed to give what I had. My body became a tool in getting what I wanted from men. Whether it was money, clothes, shoes, etc. My mind was at a disturbing turn in that time in my life. I started to hate myself, I hated my looks, and I hated my life. I wanted to die everyday and I actually tried to kill myself many times.

I tried with many pills, As I mentioned earlier, I tried again a second time, to take my life. This time I was asking people to shoot me in the head. Now the guys I was asking that thought I was just talking out of the side of my mouth, as if I was drunk. I started to drink almost every day. I kept myself full of liquor to zone out the voices that were in my head. I was never diagnosed as being bipolar, but I believe I was. I tried telling stories to people so they will get mad and kill me. I even one day tried standing in the road hoping to get hit by a car. I felt also that my body was so abused and used up that my woman parts were all worn out and would never be able to operate the way they needed to.

LOST MYSELF IN

FAKENESS

As I looked in the mirror, I never saw nice perky breasts. I didn't see myself having a tight, firm vagina. I saw a woman with a body worn out, torn up, bruised up, used up to never to come back to normal. I wanted to rearrange how I looked. Many times, I would cut my hair to look different. I changed my hair color so I wouldn't look like that girl. I even at times wanted to become a guy so I would tape down my breasts. I was even thinking of engaging in lesbian affairs. I was in a world of confusion from the moon and back.

The very first time I tried to commit suicide, I was 16 and I took a full #60 bottle of pain pills with 20/20 liquor. I wanted to die to this world because I felt that my life was already destroyed, and nothing was going to become of it. I never looked to live pass the age 18. I never thought I would have kids. I never thought I would ever get married. I just thought all bad things about myself and that no one would like or love me because of my past. You may be asking, "Well why you didn't tell the police at this time with all these things that happened to you?" I was at a point in my life that I thought the police would laugh at me and not believe me either. See, at this point I didn't trust anyone.

GIVE ME THE STRENGTH LORD TO

LOVE ALL THREE AGAIN...

Although I was dealing with some very bad dudes in my life,

I never quite felt secure with telling things that were going on with

me. I never told my boyfriend from the projects, the guy from the

gang that I was affiliated with, nor my friends. I felt as if I was in

this world on my own with no one to cry to, no one to vent to, and

no one to trust. For a long time I blamed myself for the many

different things that I encountered. I blamed myself for the rapes,

I said to myself, "If I was a pretty girl, it wouldn't have happened to me". I blamed myself for my brother getting killed in the streets because I said to myself if I had never told about my father he would had been there for the boys and been a father to them instead of them going to the streets.

Can you imagine how the household was that I lived in? We all were in gangs or affiliated with rival gangs. There were actually like four different gangs rivaling in the household. I remember when my little brother who passed told me that my gang friends better not come to the house, or it will be a war. I mean it was that serious for us to stand for what we thought was our grounds.

NO UNITY...

One kid in a Grape Street (purple) gang, one affiliated with the 6 Duce(blue and orange) gang, three kids affiliated with the 19th Street Rolling Sixties (blue and yellow)gang, and a gang that my little sisters made up: The Duchee girls. It was crazy and now that I'm grown, this was just plain old silly. We ALL could have lost our lives trying to be something we really weren't. This was the result of not having a father in the house and a single parent mother trying her best to provide and protect 7 children (4 boys, 3 girls).

Although we had our differences, we stood up for each other in the streets. We had a family fight one night. My mom once again was at church with my baby sister. I had no idea what was going on. I just had my first newborn daughter (literally a new-born), and two of my friends were walking to my house to get some clothes for me to spend the night over one of my friend's house. My daughter was at her father's house. My brother started telling me how this young girl was talking about my mother. Now this is so silly and foolish; although I had my issues with my mother, everyone knew not to talk about her or it would be a problem. My brother knew that. So while on the porch he had two by fours, pipes, bats and things like that and giving it to us to fight with. So I saw the girl walking and I ran towards her to fight her with the pole.

NO FUTURE...

Before I knew it, everyone was fighting! All my brothers, and my little sister, my friends and even a few people in the neighborhood. We all jumped on the family of the young lady who my brother told me was talking about my mom. I remember running up on her mom. Now, remember when I told you I had some strong hate for older women.

I was about to smash her head in, and something came over me not to harm her. I started to turn one way, and I felt a bang in my head but didn't realize what happened. One of the girls who we were fighting, had stabbed me in my head with a knife. Then she tried to run away and my brother caught her and slammed her to the ground. He then yelled at me to smash her face. I still never knew why. I just couldn't see myself hitting anyone in the face with a pole.

While he was yelling at me to hit her, I was telling him I can't hit her with this. My friend went to slap her in the face with a two by four. It was just crazy that night. While my mother was at church praising God, we were acting a fool at her house. Someone called the police, and I ran, blood going down my face still not realizing that I have been stabbed. When I got to my friend's grandmother's house is when I knew, and she took care of me. I just had my daughter maybe a week ago before this happened.

A BUCKET OF SUNSHINE,

I WISH...

I have been in jail a few times. As I mentioned earlier, I had

this boyfriend that lived in the Cochran Projects. Well every little

girl down there didn't want me bothering their guys in the village.

I got into so many altercations about coming down there and being

with him. As time went on, I eventually got pregnant by him with

my first daughter. I thought of him as my property, and I wasn't

going to let no one interfere with that. He had another girl

pregnant at the same time and had a baby previous. So, I got into arguments and fights with his other baby mothers. One day we all went to jail for fighting. All three of us arrested for disturbing the peace.

I also went to jail (St. Louis City Jail) at the time, for my little sister. I was 16 years old going to the big jail. I never went to Juvenile, I was always sent to the city jail. I had been in this jail three times. I thought this was the worst thing I ever experienced. No, my mom never bailed me out, and I had to spend the time they gave me there. I don't blame her at all because I just didn't stop getting into trouble.

FLOWERS AND A HEALED

HEART, I WISH...

It was a never ending story for me. I now have 3- 1st degree assault charges on my record. I wish I could turn back time, because your criminal record NEVER goes away.

I really hope I haven't lost you. I just want you to see some of the ways that people who are emotionally wounded, act out. It contributes to other things in their lives. I became a product of my community and circumstance. I was heartless and cruel, full of hate and anger. I was a walking time bomb, ready to blow at any given second. I built a wall up for myself to protect me, because no one else had. I thought I was my own god at that point, feeling I had the right to life and death in my hands.

Chapter 9

When I got pregnant with my first daughter at the age 17, I remember I told my mom and she laughed. She told me I was lying. I'm not sure even to this day what that was all about, but evidentially I wasn't. I was pregnant. I was seriously feeling like running away. I never wanted to have kids, especially girls. I wasn't sure if I could give them the love that they needed. I didn't know what love was or yet how to give it.

When I was 8 months pregnant, I was on my way to the clinic to check on my baby. One of the guys who I was having problems with from a rival gang pulled up on the bus stop. He made a U-turn to jump out the car, with a gun pointed to my belly.

FOR MY 4 CHILDREN...

I remember the whole conversation. It happened so fast but it was so scary too. As he was driving and saw me and shouted, "Now what Bitch? Where your boys at now?" I didn't say anything back because I was by myself on the bus stop. He made a U-turn and literally jumped out the car and pointed the gun to my belly. I stood there in shock and tears started to run down my face. His friend said "Dude what are you doing she is pregnant?" and he hit the gun from the guy hand and yelled at me to run. Thank God, his friend got out the car and tackled him to the ground. He took the gun from him, and told me to run. I ran as fast as I could. I remember people were asking me if I was alright and stop running before I fall. I ran home so fast, you would have thought I was on a track team. I still never told anyone. I just went on that day as if nothing ever happened. I was good at pretending that things were good when they weren't. Whew! That was like the beginning of the end for me in so many ways than one.

Even though I had this child, my child, I was still getting into trouble. I was still walking around trying to start fights with other ladies. I few ladies came to my house one morning again and threatened me with a gun pointed to my head. They told me to stay away from their territory. They went on to say they heard about me, my friends, and they "will end it for us". *****Whew that was like the beginning of the end for me in so many ways than one*****

LOVE DANGLING ON THE

VINE OF HOPE...

At this time, my mom finally had to move from that area on the north side of St. Louis in the Bremen park area. I was so happy because truth be told, I was tired of this life that I was making for myself and now my daughter. I wanted, needed a change of scenery.

Now I'm about to keep moving on in this crazy life cycle of my youth. My daughter is at the age 1, and I just got into a bad fight with some guys the night before and they seriously beat me up. I never went to the hospital. I doctored on myself. While I was pouring peroxide on wounds that were open, I was crying asking this God that I heard my mother talk to if He can help me. I remember saying, "If you are real, find a way for me to get out this crap I put myself in".

Maybe a few days later, I decided to go to church with my mom. I wasn't going to find a boyfriend or anything like that. I was single and glad about it. I needed help, and I was just thinking this is my last resort…for real. I remember asking my mom, yes my mom, if me and the baby could go to church with her. She told me I couldn't, but that she would take the baby. I thought, "What is the problem with this lady?" Does she even care about why I need to go to church? Does she even know what happened to me the night before and that I'm on the edge right now?

FOR ALL THOSE THAT CAN'T SPEAK

ON THEIR PAIN...

As the church van pulled up to pick her up with my daughter, I ran out the door and jumped in the van. I knew she would not tell me to get out in front of the pastor. With that step, this started my journey to going back to church.

I have been going to church all my life, even when I was staying with my grandmother. While living with her, I was attending the Salvation Church in Wellston. I went to the church up until I was age 15. That's when I met the "man" who really took my virginity; he didn't rape me. The was the first older guy I actually wanted to sleep with. He was the main reason why I choose to deal with older men instead of younger men. He was 21 and I was 15 at the time. I never lied about my age to any of the guys I slept with, and they seem to care. The older men were the ones who brought me clothes, shoes, jewelry and etc. Now, you see why I used my body to get what I want, even though it wasn't a good thing to do. The situation I was in with the older men molded my mind to want to do it.

I was thinking now that I'm not a virgin anymore, this will be the time of my life.

WHERE IS GOD REALLY?

Although I was thinking to do one thing with my body, now that I'm not a virgin any longer however other horrible things started happening to me as a mentioned earlier.

What I wanted from going to my mom's church was some help. I was all wiped out from trying to help myself. I was all helped out for myself. I didn't know where else to turn and I felt if I didn't get this help from church, that I was literally going to die in these streets. I didn't want to have to leave my child to no one else. You may be saying right now that, "Yes, she finally got help!" Nope. It didn't end that easy.

Chapter 10

I met my first ex-husband at church. We were dating for 4 years, before we became husband and wife (now that's another book.) That was a terrible marriage, and it ended horribly.

Yes, I was going to church every single time the doors were open, and I loved it. I got married and that same husband did the unthinkable to me. He cheated right under my nose. Not with just one girl, but many. His cousins were trying to warn me about him, but I didn't believe it. My brother, the one who died, also tried to warn me. I didn't believe him when he came to tell me some things about my husband at the time, he stopped talking to me. So my brother died, not knowing how much I loved him and that I appreciated him. I began to have hate in my heart towards my ex-husband because he was actually the reason my brother stopped talking to me. Our marriage was going downhill. Now, in no way does that excuse why he was having multiple affairs on me.

I'm going to jump ahead for a moment, bear with me. I was not healed and totally delivered form the harm of men in my life.

I'M STILL LOOKING FOR

THIS GOD...

When my ex-husband started to do things like cheat, not take care of the home, spent money on himself and not the kids, he eventually left me. He left me and my daughters homeless.

When we were married, the first year it was a disaster. Just like any other situation in my life dealing with men, I had no help.

I HAD NO HELP.

I KNEW THERE WAS AN ANGEL

SOMEWHERE CARRYING MY

HEART...

His parents knew everything I was going through with their

son but wouldn't help me in this situation. I had to deal with

women coming to my house to pick him up. I was dealing with

these same women coming to the same church I attended with my husband. I would be sitting on one side of the church with my kids, and he and his girlfriends would be on the other side. I forgot to tell you, he had other children inside our marriage union. I was just dealing with a bunch of shenanigans. I remember one of the baby mothers' telling me that the parents use to try to hide her when I came to their home.

No one, not even the pastors, would ask me how I felt about the situation. I was always told I was the 'strong one' and 'just hold on'. What kind of mess was that? But his parents told me this, so what did I expect?

Some time before I got married, I became ill. I woke up one morning with a tumor the size of a grapefruit hanging from the side of my neck on the left side. During this time I became sick with an illness that effected my throat, neck, shoulder and head, it was what was called a Desmoid tumor. These are very rare tumors and only about 1 out of 20,000 will come up with this tumor. It's not hereditary or anything like that.

At this very time of the sickness I got married and had to have 2 surgeries to remove the tumor from both sides of my neck. The first surgery lasted 8 hours because it was the size of a grapefruit and crushing my vocal cord and take note that I was 6 months pregnant with my second daughter. The second surgery last an hour because it was caught early and was small. I went through chemo for two months during pregnancy and 4 months of radiation after pregnancy.

LEARNING TO TRUST THIS

GOD...

After we got married, I then went to have surgery while I was pregnant with my second daughter (whom was his), this surgery lasted for 8 hrs. After the surgery, I still had some of the tumor left in me and needed to be worked on more because of the placement. My husband was still running around on me, which left me to take care of two babies at the same time I'm ill going back and forth to the hospital getting radiation treatments and chemo to shrink the tumor. Now you would have thought that the people in the other church would have my back by them being my friends and they knew what was going on. Well, that didn't happen. I was told by a friend that if I was to stay at the church I had to suck it up about my HUSBAND coming to church with another woman. I didn't know what to do about that so I left that church too.

I would be sitting on one side of the church with my kids and he and his girlfriends would be on the other side. I remember one of the baby mothers's telling me that his parents use to try to hide her when I came to their home. Oh I forgot to tell you that he had other babies inside our marriage union. I was just dealing with a bunch of shenanigans. No one not even the pastors would ask me how I felt about the situation but I was always told I was the strong one and just hold on. Hold on to what? This boy just wasn't TAUGHT how to be a man.

JUST PICKING UP THE

PIECES AND TRYING TO FIT

THEM PERFECTLY...

With all this going on the unthinkable happened to me. I LATER had to find out that my husband, at the time, had been sleeping around with one of my good friends since the beginning, we were just dating and it lasted all the way through our marriage and after the divorce for around 10 years.

I was told that while she was spending nights at my house, they would go down stairs in my basement and have sex. They would go to the park with friends and go off and have sex. The whole time we were dating, married, having out problems and even during the divorce I confided with her and cried to her and at the same time was having sex with my husband right under my nose. Oh the hurt and pain I ENGAGED. I STILL FEEL AS IF SHE DOESN'T CARE ABOUT WHAT SHE DID.

DEALING WITH LOW SELF-ESTEEM

After around the 5th year of being married but living separate, I felt as if I was keeping myself for what? I had seen my husband get away with doing things to me, so why am I trying to be the 'nice girl'? Here I go again walking in defeat, just to encounter a stronger demon that was waiting to lift me up in his arms. So who

was close to me to see my pain and help me to become devious?

The men in the church, who I seen every day. I slept with a few

pastors and other men in the body of Christ. I felt as if there was

no hope in trying to do right at the moment. So yes, I did it.

The wounded heart from

friends...

The cycle started once again. I started to lose myself, not

caring for myself once again. I ran across men in the church, who would tell me lies about how they cared for me or I would have pastors lying on me and to me. These pastors called me 'whore,' and that I was making their church look bad. As if it took one person to have sex. It was because of his family who I slept with at that time, he dare not to turn on the man since I was the adulterous woman. He also said that I should have been stoned to death just like the women in the Bible were. I even had a pastor to make his whole church turn against me with his accusations. He told them to watch their husbands around me because I was a 'seductress'. With me getting drawn into depression again I became what that pastor said: a seductress. Not only that, I became that person who I despised: an adulterous woman.

STARTED TO BECOME MY OWN

MONSTER...

The pastor probably seen it but didn't have the compassion to pray and help me to be removed from it...**A SEDUCTRESS.**

And not only that I became that person who I despised...

AN ADULTRESS***

I slept with friends' husbands because of the hurt that was in me, hating them that they wouldn't stop a hurt that would overtake me. I slept with other women husbands who I didn't know however the disgust and shame never over looked me. I was full of shame and hurt to be a person who I said I would never be.

Dealing with the many men in the church was like putting a knife in my heart, and turning it around to not pull it out. Once again, I put my trust in these men only to know that they only used my hurts to defile me in the end. Do I still have these issues with men? Do I still see those pastors and other men? Yes, I do. This healing process has been long and overdue. And now I'm surrounded by women in the church who dislike me because of what others tell them? Now there are men in the church who see the hurt and pain in me but because of their own insecurities they were willing to use a wounded soul such as myself? *This has left me in being spiritually raped.*

THE SPIRIT OF JEZEBEL

It took a while for me to trust these godly men again but that doesn't mean I forgot. I just forgave. Now don't get me wrong men in churches are also men of the flesh. They are not perfect and they too make mistakes just as other men.

Dealing with the pain from second husband

Now remember the dude from the projects that I was seeing and got my first daughter by? Well, he came back into my life during the time of the LONG separation from my first husband. Once again I was over taken by the love and compassion the he was showing me at the time. He moved in with me and about a year into the relationship we decided to get married. Right after I FINALLY divorced my first husband after staying married for 6 LONG years.

This young man was the world to me and my two girls during this short time we were together. He came in washing clothes, cooking dinner, giving me his WHOLE work check, only asking for cigarettes (lol), took the kids to school. I literally didn't have to do a thing but go to work myself, come home sleep and eat. After divorcing my first husband I married him and became pregnant with my baby girl...

ANGEL WATCHING OVER

ME...

However he also was hiding a demon within himself that I didn't know about. He was on drugs. That became a problem for us. The physical abuse started. The last straw was when the gun was introduced in the relationship. I was done with him maybe about the 6 month into our marriage. I put him out of my house and I was sleeping with this other guy. Well one day he decided to do right by me and I just wanted to be honest about everything that I had done. I told him about the affair I had and he flipped out as I thought was going to happen. So many things happened but this one thing that happened crushed my inner heart. He raped me.

I know people are saying that husbands cannot rape their wives, well that is so not true. Yes, they can. My sheets were full of blood and I was telling him that he was hurting me but he didn't care. During the time of raping me, he held a gun to my head telling me to not scream for the children. I knew he was high off drugs at the time. I was only wishing and praying that the day would end.

He finally fell asleep with the gun on the floor next to him and this was the time I really experience the war within. One side telling me to kill him and the other side was telling me to just walk away. Now before this incident happened other things happened. He shook my house to pieces and at that moment I needed to get me and my children out of this lifestyle before there be a murder on hand. So I eventually divorced him also.

Chapter 11

Now just to tell you a lil story about some other church people. These people were actually my family. Yes my biological family and a husband's family through marriage. Even in the midst of all the things I did in the church I made it my business to give God all that I have. Now I am a very creative person. For some reason I always had problems with the family members that were going to church with me. Every time I looked around this uncle, through marriage would start trouble between me and his daughters and even between his wife, who is the sister of my father. My 2 girl cousins would try to start fights with me for no reason. They would lie on me to start problems. When my brother died these were the same cousins that I had to fight because they came to my mom home starting trouble.

Yes I actually got into a physical fight with two of my cousins in the church and with everything that went on between the three of us, I had always tried to love them in spite of the wrong that they did to me but there just seem like I was wasting time. There was a lot of jealousy that I was encountering with the cousins and their dad and it was just becoming too much to deal with even in the church. Yes, but it's gets easier to deal with every day.

I'M SEARCHING FOR THIS

ANGEL

It took a while for me to trust these men again, but that doesn't mean I forgot. I forgave. Now don't get me wrong. Men in

DIARY OF A WOUNDED WOMAN

churches are also men of the flesh. They are not perfect and they too make mistakes just as other men. Let me tell you a little story about some other church people I was with in the church. These people were actually my family. Yes, my natural family and family through marriage. Even in the midst of all the things I did in the church, I made it my business to give God all that I had.

I am a very creative person. For some reason, I always had problems with the family members that were going to church with me. Every time I looked around, this uncle (through marriage) would start trouble between me and his children. Even between me and his wife, who is the sister of my father. He had stopped us from doing things together pertaining to the church. He had even gone so far to tell the pastor I was under at the time, that if he wouldn't put me out the church that him and his family would leave. I didn't get put out the church. You guessed it, the family left the church. This man has always had it out for me. I have no idea why but he is part of the pain that must be addressed. It's just so funny to me how these men called me god-daughter, favorite niece and spiritual daughter would hate me in the inside. I struggled so hard to date (even now), to love those that evidently don't have any for me. I had failed at that, many times.

Chapter 12

I'm jumping over again; let me take you back a few years before I started to go back to church. I hadn't yet left my mom's house. I started going to college, I also was working. I planned to stayed with my mom till I finished school as I had hoped. Everything was going well as it could be. Yes, we as siblings had our own issues here and there. We still fought in the streets, but I was looking to change for the better. Well, one day as I was heading home, I opened the door to hearing this man in our home. It was my father. He had got out of jail and my mother never bothered to tell me about this. I was so mad at her, I was full of emotions because for 1 thing he didn't spend his whole time in jail, and then my mom keeping secrets!

I had to deal with this man getting out of jail early, and on top of that he was trying to control me and the things I was doing. As I mentioned a little back I was dating this guy for 4 years, who was my 1st husband (and first ex-husband). My father thought he had the right to say something to me about having male company. I was starting to feel that he was jealous of my boyfriend. That's crazy I thought, but it was how I was feeling. I believe it with all my heart that it was the truth.

ANGEL OF DARKNESS

ENTERED...

This man tried to become a dad that was dead to me along with other men I have encountered in my life. My mom protected him at any cost. I tried to kill this man on many occasions.

My mom would jump in the middle of us to break it up. I was

starting to feel that he was jealous of my boyfriend. This man tried

to become a dad that was dead to me along with other men I have

encountered in my life and my mom protected him at any cost. I

tried to kill him and my mom would defend him and instead of

yelling at him she would yell at me and put me out the house.

This was the beginning of me hating my mom.

MY ANGEL TIRED OF

PROTECTING ME...

Now that this man was out of jail, he seemed not to want to rebuild the family and start brand new. He still wanted to destroy the lives of his children, and my mother helped him. I'm not going to sit here like I had everything all together. I don't. I'm still struggling with loving my mom the way I'm supposed to. I feel like she protects that demon in him and not care about her children that she birthed. My father is sick and he needs a doctor, not this human doctor, but Jesus Christ. That demon in him is out to destroy any and every one that is involved with him.

I have tried to talk to my mom and ask her what was she thinking with all this. It's hard when she is constantly protecting a man who has no heart for his family. I take that back; he has heart for some of his kids. As for me? He told me personally that he hated me, and wished I was never born. When I was like 19 years old, I did approach him and asked him why he hurt me like he did. His response was, "I was mad at your mother." He never said he was sorry. HE NEVER SAID "I'M SORRY."

He never said sorry.

SHE'S STANDING WAITING

My mother always was quick to say I had a demon inside me but never wanted to deal with the real issues at hand. I never dealt with my father's side of the family because two of my aunts kept their daughters away from me. They said I was a bad influence on their children. But the two cousins I was kept away from were the two who got pregnant BEFORE I did but I was the bad influence. Just so sad to say that I never had a real relationship with my family. I had literally no one to confide in or even turn to talk with.

This was why "I" was the main factor of my life.

TRYING TO HEAR SWEET

SOUNDS...

I love my mother with what I have left in me, but I don't know how to show the love without the hurt feelings all coming back to hurt. Even to this day and time my mother is still married and lives with my father. Even with everything that has happened, everything extra that had gone on, she still sees it to be the best for her to stay with this man, my father. I just don't know how to explain it; she says God never told her to leave him.

I don't know about that because God, the God I serve, also loves family. HE is all about the restoration and healing of family. If someone is not trying to help with the process of healing, and you keep telling me that the same God that I serve and that you serve, will still tell you not to leave this demon? I just don't know about that.

MY MOUTH BECAME A

LETHAL WEAPON...

I wrote my mom a letter one year ago about our relationship and here it is. I'm not sure if she will ever understand the pain and hurt that was embedded in me from her and her husband. The purpose of the letter was to tell her and hopefully have her understand the part that she played in it. To tell her why things were the way it was between the both of us. It was a love-hate relationship between me and my mother. I loved her because she is my mother. I hate her for not being the one to protect me and love on me the way a mother is suppose to love her children.

I always felt even up til now that she blames me for a lot of things. I never understood why she stayed with the very man who brought harm to her children even to this day… THIS LETTER IS A PART OF THE BOOK BECAUSE MANY DIDN'T KNOW THAT THIS WAS DURING THE TIME OF A BREAKDOWN THAT WAS TRYING TO TAKE OVER ME. BUT GOD CAME IN AND RESCUED ME ONCE AGAIN.

I have deleted some names.

Friday September 19, 2014

1: 00 p.m.

Dear Mother,

I am writing because I have a lot of issues on my heart and I must release these issues. I have never been able to actually tell you of the hurt and how I feel without anger coming out. I have tried to just go on my days and put these issues behind me but every day is a great torture for me and I REFUSE TO ALLOW MY ISSUES FROM THE PAST TO TAKE OVER MY HOME WITH MY CHILDREN. Making me an angry individual because of the choices others has made.

My heart goes out for you. I don't think you quite understand the role that you play in the dysfunction of this family. We can go on for so long like nothing is bothering us but it is. You need to own up to the responsibility that you have in this hurt. You have never owned up to it. You keep saying you made a mistake. A mistake is when you do a thing and you DO NOT KNOW THAT IT IS THE WRONG THING TO DO. You knew what you were doing and it sometimes feel as if you didn't care about how it would affect your children, especially those that was wounded from your husband. So that is not a mistake that is a doing what I want to do act.

I was molested by your husband for 6 years and he attempted to rape me at the age of 11. If it wasn't for my little brother busting in the door, he would have succeeded. Do you have any idea of the hurt that it was to see my father hurt me and when I tell you what he had done, you did nothing about it? You believed him. To know that he came into my room that very night again despite me telling his wife of what he was doing to me! This is one of the many pains that are so hard to get over. Especially, when you don't take the time out of your busy schedule to make things right.

Then on top of me trying to deal with siblings who blame me for the reason why he wasn't in the home, I felt that you also blamed me for your husband not being there. I never said anything because I was always under the impression that you don't care.

Then you sent me to his mother home, DO YOU HAVE ANY IDEA OF THE THINGS I HAD TO GO THROUGH IN THAT HOUSE? THE MANY NAME CALLING, THE MANY LIES THAT WERE BEING TOLD ON ME, THE MANY DAYS WHEN I DIDN'T EAT BECAUSE THIS LADY WAS IN ONE OF HER MOODS ABOUT ME WITH HER SON. Do you even know about the time your husband came to his mom house and he tried to make me sit on his lap? His brothers never intervened that. His sisters treated me like I was an outcast. That's why I hated them! God found a way for me and one of my aunt to mend our differences before she died. I pray that will be the same with the other sisters, but if not I refuse to live another day worrying about what they think, and how they feel towards me.

Another thing I need your to recognize is if you had to obeyed the system, and not allow that man in the home, your daughter would not have gone through what she had. You kept that a secret. You knew that it would have done something to me, especially with me having a daughter at that time. You were okay with letting him in the home with your daughters even with a daughter that he has harmed, physically and sexually.

You have no idea of the many things I had gone through just because I was told 'this is what you must do in order for a man to love you'. I didn't hear that for any random man. I heard that from my father! This pain is hard and until you have been through what I been through, you will never understand the pain. So you might be saying that Jesus is a healer and deliverer . HE forgives our past. Yes, this is all true. What you need to understand is everything is a process and the process is painful. People also must accept the responsibility of what they have done in the harm of an individual.

I am not asking you to forgive me. I am sorry, you actually don't think you did anything wrong, and I am fully aware of that. I am aware just by listening to your reaction in the conversation two Saturdays ago. You tried to play the victim role saying 'we don't know how you feel'.

YOU DON'T UNDERSTAND THIS IS NOT ABOUT YOU! YOUR FEELINGS ARE IRRELEVANT TO THE

PROBLEM. YOU ALLOW THE SCAB TO BE REOPENED WHEN YOU ALLOWED HIM TO COME BACK INTO MY LIFE WITHOUT EVEN GIVING ME A CHANCE TO HEAL.

You are so quick to sweep things under the rug and not deal with what needs to be dealt with. My kids are NEVER ALLOWED TO YOUR HOME AND I WILL NEVER GO BACK INTO YOUR HOME. THAT HOME BELONGS TO YOU AND YOUR HUSBAND. I don't trust you to protect my children from him. I am not like you. He will not get away with that with my kids. I don't trust him around my kids either.

This is so sad to say but I REALLY NEED TIME AWAY FROM YOU RIGHT NOW. I DON'T KNOW HOW LONG I NEED, BUT I KNOW I NEED IT. IT HURTS ME DEEPLY TO BE THIS WAY BUT I THINK THE ONLY WAY HEALING WILL BEGIN FOR ME, IS TO GET TO KNOW MYSELF AND WORK ON ME MORE. I NEED TO NOT BE IN THE PRESENCE OF THE ONES THAT HAVE HURT ME. EVERYONE DEALS WITH THINGS DIFFERENT. SO DON'T

COME TELLING ME I HAVEN'T FORGIVEN BECAUSE I DON'T WANT TO BE AROUND YOU. I KNOW ME AND THE CONVERSATION WILL ALWAYS COME UP UNTIL YOU ACKNOWLEDGE YOUR PART. SO, TO NOT HURT YOUR FEELINGS I WILL JUST STAY WAY UNTIL "GOD" SAYS IT'S OKAY NOW.

YOU CANNOT THINK THAT EVERYTHING IS JUST SUPPOSED TO BYPASS ME, AND I WILL START ACTING THE SAME WHEN THE BANDAGE WAS LIFTED OFF THE SORE. I KNOW THAT NIGHT WAS PREDESTINDED TO HAPPEN BECAUSE IT WAS NEEDED FOR US TO SEE AND HEAR WHAT WAS SAID.

Whatever I must go through I will go through it with the help of the Lord. You need to know that we love you so much and it hurts us to act the way we do when things come up. You have never sat down to talk with us and to let us know that you understand our hurt, and that you plan to make a difference. Have you ever had a love-hate feeling for someone and it hurt you to feel that way? That's what I feel towards you.

I love you, but I also hate you for not protecting me and taking the time to help me heal. You say that your husband loves you. How and why would you say something like that to children that HE HATE?! Mom, you need to know what it means to love someone and he does not love you. I don't know what he has over you, or what kind of bondage that he has put you in, but I do pray that you repent from the wrong that you have done.

You say what is it that you need to do? And that God did not tell you to leave him. I'm not sure what God you are serving, because the same God that you claim to serve, and that I serve, tells me and open doors for me to get away from no good men. They didn't do to my daughters as your husband did to yours, and you say God didn't tell you to leave. NOPE I DON'T BELEIVE OR UNDERSTAND THAT GOD.

THIS IS MY PRAYER THAT MY HEART GETS TOTALLY HEALED AND THAT I UNDERSTAND YOU AND YOUR DECISIONS:

There is so much more that I can say, but I feel in my spirit that I need to stop right here. I know time will heal all wounds and I am truly looking forward to that day when my Lord will heal my broken heart and replace it with love and compassion for all that have hurt me.

THAT'S ALL I HAVE TO SAY..

THIS TOO SHALL PASS.

Sincerely,

Shanta

This letter was not what I wanted it to be, it sent out the wrong vibes. My older brother, yes my brother has stopped talking to me because of finding out about the letter and not understanding were I was coming from in writing the letter. He said I was to get over it. Yeah, that would come out of his mouth. I have other family members choosing not to deal with me because of my life exposure. My nieces, nephew and others who just simply don't understand this is my life that has been surrounded by hatred, resentment, bitterness, anger, low self-esteem, loneliness, lies, and shame.

BEGINNING OF THE DRUG USE...

I was seeing a psychiatrist for 4 years (2007-2011), I was diagnosed as having PTSD and took Prozac for depression. For another round, I was seeing a therapist for 2 years (2013-2015). I was diagnosed as having extreme depression with the degree of Bipolar II. I have fallen under the statistics of over-the-counter drug addiction.

I became immune to hardships and thought that it was the way to live. I suffer from suicidal thoughts even now AND I fall easily into depression and I know this about myself so I have found ways to deal with life issues on my own. I tell people, "My help is only in God. But God". This is my life that needs to be glued back as a whole, so I can live and not just exist. I can breathe correctly. With it all written down, I haven't even realized how much I been through, and I haven't even began to scratch the surface yet.

The purpose of the letter was to help her understand where I was coming from with all the bitterness I was holding and allowing to take over me for so many years. Now, I choose to get free entirely. You all may be saying, "Wow, Shanta! That's a lot of stuff you are exposing". This is only the surface of things that I have been dealing with. I'm sorry if this may be too much for you all to understand, and even to those who know what I'm talking about. You may feel some sort of way about my recovery book.

I fully understand that this may be a lot for you to digest but I promise you there is a light at the end of the tunnel. So you may be wondering, "So Shanta how did you really get over the things that you went through and people that have wronged you?" It may sound like a cliché but I promise you it WORKS... I prayed and cried out to the Lord Jesus Christ. Now I try not to dictate who your God is, but I am a true believer of Jesus Christ. He, who was born of a virgin, died a crucial and terrible death just for people like you and I. He rose on the third day to let us know that NOTHING CAN OVERTAKE US in this world not even death.. He is truly an awesome God. I cried out to him almost daily, some days were easier than others. I cried for the healing of my heart because I was just tired of being full of anger, bitterness and disgust... I have loss friendships because of my nasty attitude. I was tired and knew in all heart that He could and want to help me.

This is my story and I was told personally by My God, Jesus Christ, to write, get set free and stay free indeed. I have tried to delete some things in this book and was only on my face in prayer telling me to put it back in the book. I'm sorry to the ones that are a part of this life in this book. I'm sorry to my mother, my father and to my brother. Once again, this is not about making any one to look bad or even for revenge. There is no such thing as revenge, there's a thing call GET SET FREE. Everyone needs to deal with their issues different, and I choose to tell my story to help those that don't have a voice for themselves. I use my voice also for those that feel trapped in a past life, can't move on and live. This is your time, ladies and gentlemen. Rise up out of your pain and decree and declare the freedom and take back your right to live and not just exist.

Closing Thoughts

I found scriptures in the Bible pertaining to my issues: bitterness, anger, hatred, fatherless, motherless, loss of sibling, insecurities and many more things. I started to speak those scriptures out daily and I just trusted Jesus to help me through everything. The dreams, the thoughts, the visions, the memories, I just believed He would do it for me. Then, my loves, I learned how to walk in my deliverance without condemnation.

So with EVERYTHING I have been through and still going through even to date, I can honestly say I thank God, Jesus Christ, the true Lord over all things. I thank Him for seeing me through it all. No everything has not been the best. But it has made me the woman that I am on this day. Would I take back my life?

NO MA'AM! I wouldn't because without the hurts and pain then I would have never met my Gracious and Loving God☺ He was there with me all the time.

I AM DELIVERED FROM BEING THAT SEDUCTRESs,
ADULTEROUS, SUICIDE, LOW SELF ESTEEM, FEARFUL,
ANGRY, BITTER, HATERED, LADY... I HAVE OVERCOME
THAT LONELINESS IN MY LIFE AND MANY MORE
THINGS☺

*****I'M STILL AT WORK AND UNDER CONSTRUCTION
TO BE WHOLE*****

PRAYER

I pray that my testimonial book will help you to overcome any and all things that surround you.

I pray that you get the voice that God has given you to speak against all abuse.

I pray that you will get the strength from God to stand for what is right.

I pray that the hearts of all those that have been wounded and hurt will start afresh in their healing.

I pray for the victims of all forms of abuse (sexual, physical emotional/spiritual) that you will find that inner super hero and save yourself with the help of God to from the bondage of shame and defeat.

With everything I have been through, still going through, I can honestly say I thank God, Jesus Christ, the true Lord over all things for seeing me through it all. No, everything has not been the best. But it has made me the woman that I am this day. Would

I take back my life? No ma'am! Why? I wouldn't because without the hurt and pain, I would have never met my gracious and loving God. HE was there with me all the time.

ALL THE GLORY BELONGS TO GOD, JESUS CHRIST, THE TRUE AND LIVING GOD OVER THEM ALL!

I AM DELIVERED FROM BEING THAT SEDUCTRESS AND ADULTEROUS LADY. I HAVE OVERCOME THAT LONELINESS IN MY LIFE AND MANY MORE THINGS.

I'M STILL AT WORK AND UNDER CONSRTUCTION TO BE WHOLE.

THE HEART IS THE ONE THING THAT MUST BE TREATED GENTLY WITH PRAYER. THE HEART IS THE ONE THING THAT LOSES ITS COLOR, BUT FUNCTONS THE SAME.

THE HEART IS THE ONE THING THAT ONE PERSON CAN FILL AND ANOTHER FEEL.

THE HEART IS THE ONE THING THAT CAN LOVE AND HATE TOGETHER.

THE HEART IS THE ONE THING THAT CAN BE CRUSHED THEN MENDED AGAIN .

What you will read now is some scriptures and songs that helped me. Let it minister to you. LET'S GET HEALED TOGETHER! I love you all and may the peace of God overtake and surpass you!

HEALING-

HEALING SONG:

"The Battle Is Not Yours" by Yolanda Adams

HEALING SCRIPTURES:

Psalm 30: 1-3:

I will extol You, O Lord, for You have lifted me up, And have not let my foes rejoice over me. O Lord my God, I cried out to You, And You healed me. O Lord, You brought my soul up from the grave; You have kept me alive, that I should not do down in the pit.

Psalm 107: 19-21:

Then they cried out to the Lord in their trouble, And He saved them out of their distress. He sent His word and healed them, And delivered them from their destructions. Oh, that men would give thanks to the Lord for His goodness, And for His wonderful works to the children of men!

Isaiah 41:10:

Fear not, for I am with you; Be not dismayed, for I am your God. I will strengthen you, Yes, I will help you, I will uphold you with My righteous right hand

FORGIVENESS:

FORGIVING SONG:

"Nobody Told Me" by Mary Mary

FORGIVING SCRIPTURES:

Matthew 6:14&15-

For if you forgive men their trespasses, your heavenly Father will also forgive you. But if you do not forgive men their trespasses,

neither will your Father forgive your trespasses.

2 Corinthians 5:17-

Therefore, if anyone is in Christ, he is a new creation; old things

have passed away; behold, all things have become new.

LOVE:

LOVE SONG:

"Alabaster Box" by CeCe Winans

LOVE SCRIPTURES:

1 John 4: 7&8:

Beloved, let us love one another, for love is of God; and everyone

who loves is born of God and knows God. He who does not love

does not know God, for God is love.

ABOUT THE AUTHOR

Ambassador for Jesus Christ Shanta Nicole Scott has been launched out into the darkness of this world for those without a voice about the hurt and harm of their lives.

She has 4 lovely children, Shantez, A'Shantee, Miracle and Caleb.

Shanta has her high school diploma from Meda P. Washington (for pregnant teens).

She later received two college degrees:

2010' Associate in Applied Science (Human Service/Social work) from Flo-Valley community college.

2013' Bachelor of Science (Christian theology/ Human Service), at the same time Shanta was given an excellent academic achievement award on the Dean's list, with a grade point average 3.602 on July 11, 2013.

Shanta received her licensed to minister in July 2012 under the leadership of Apostle Gregory Holley and Pastor Diane Holley, Grace Fellowship church.

She later was ordained as an associate Pastor under the leadership of the same Pastors at Grace Fellowship in September 2013. Shanta had the privilege to be the spiritual teacher of dance over 15 years with over 30 ladies of the ages 2 on up. Later became the spiritual mentor group by the name Sista2Sista for young ladies for 4 years. She also produced (2) Spiritual mock weddings. She was also the producer of many spiritual plays, skits and monologue...

A woman who wants to be used by God, Jesus Christ.